I'm Jack. I'm black.

ISBN: 978-0-9894764-8-5

Different hair
Different skin
Different outside
Same within

Different language
Different name
In our hearts
All the same

-T.Jackson

To my angel in Heaven & my angel on Earth

To Trayvon and Amadou and Emmett

I'm Jack.
I'm black.

Written and illustrated
by Toney Jackson

Hi! I'm Jack.

I'm black.

I love being black!

Black is

Black like shadows,

and ladybug spots.

Black like skies at night.

Some people
don't like black.

Some people
are scared of me.

They cross the street
to get away from me.

They say I'm bad luck.

My friend Max
thinks black is beautiful.

He doesn't care
what people say.

He knows I'm nice,

and fun,

and cool.

I know there are more people like Max.

I hope to meet them and make more friends!

Maybe when they meet me

they will see...

black is

beautiful!

I'm not bad,

or scary,

or unlucky.

I'm just a cat.

Toney Jackson loves learning! He loves learning so much that he became a teacher. As a teacher he helps others learn, and he learns from them as well. He loves to read, write, rap, run, eat, cook, watch cartoons and go on adventures. Toney lives in New Jersey with his wife Danielle, their daughter Jillian, and their two cats Ceri and Jack. Toney also loves to make new friends, like you! Hi friend!

Connect with Toney!
www.toneyjackson.com
Email: jacksontoney@gmail.com
Twitter & Instagram:
@HeRhymesWithMe